World War II
in
Cartoons

First published in 2009. A catalogue record for this book is available from the British Library

ISBN 978-1-844258-43-7

Published by Haynes Publishing, Sparkford, Yeovil, Somerset BA22 7JJ, UK
Tel: 01963 442030 Fax: 01963 440001 Int. tel: +44 1963 442030 Int. fax: +44 1963 440001
E-mail: sales@haynes.co.uk Website: www.haynes.co.uk

Haynes North America Inc., 861 Lawrence Drive, Newbury Park, California 91320, USA

All images © Mirrorpix

Creative Director: Kevin Gardner

Design and Artwork: David Wildish

Packaged for Haynes by Green Umbrella Publishing

Printed and bound in Britain by J F Print Ltd., Sparkford, Somerset

World War II
in
Cartoons

Written By Christopher Tiffney

Foreword

In the dark days of the Second World War, humour played its part in the defence of Britain and continued to lift the spirits of those left behind on the home front. The skill of cartoonists in distilling the events into graphic form was extraordinary, and provides us with a contemporaneous view of the war. It's not perception honed by the benefit of hindsight, but one formed in "the now" with, in some cases, personal fears and observations shining through. The cartoons collected here illustrate many of the major events and issues of the war. This is not intended to be a comprehensive history of the conflict, nor are all the cartoons either politically correct or historically accurate; but that is not their point.

As Britain faced her darkest hour, the lampooning of Hitler and his cohorts with caricatures and their portrayal as a bunch of deluded no-hopers helped to bolster the spirits of the population. An enemy you can laugh at isn't nearly as scary. The national mood can be plotted through these cartoons: fear, defiance, suffering, determination, pride, hope, relief and jubilation are all reflected in these pages.

The bravery and sacrifice of the millions of men and women who brought about the defeat of Hitler and his regime is beyond description. This book is dedicated to them.

> "Life does not cease to be funny when people die any more than it ceases to be serious when people laugh."
>
> **George Bernard Shaw**

Note: *The dates shown for each cartoon are those of publication. This was often some time after the event in question.*

The effects of the blast caused by the explosion from a V2 rocket attack on North London 1944.

3rd September 1939, crowds gathered outside the Houses of
Parliament awaiting news of the ultimatum given to Germany.
Shortly after 11am Prime Minister Neville Chamberlain announced
that Britain was at war.

ONWARD !

3rd September 1939

In May 1939 Italy under Benito Mussolini had thrown its weight behind Hitler by agreeing the "Pact of Steel". This was followed by Russia agreeing a pact of non-aggression with Germany in August. Hitler believed that Germany was now unbeatable and that Britain would not act if he invaded Poland. His tanks rolled into Poland on 1st September 1939. On 3rd September Britain declared war on Germany.

17th September 1939

Even in the early stages of the war the German people suffered shortages of food and other goods as all their country's resources were poured into the military effort. While at times they benefited from looted or expropriated goods, the wartime lot of the German civilian population was not an easy one. It was perhaps a small consolation to the British people who survived on so little that the enemy was faring no better.

Strength—Through Joy!

18th September 1939

The world had watched Hitler's Germany pursue its violently expansionist ambitions for some time with bated breath. Now what had been coming was finally under way; the Second World War had started. After witnessing the violence of Hitler's first invasions, the Nazi slogan "Strength through Joy" was sounding rather ludicrous to non-Nazi ears.

24th September 1939

Towards the end of the war Hitler's erratic decisions and bizarre behaviour led most observers to believe that he was insane. But even at the outbreak of the war many observers felt his invasion of Poland, which he thought would bring about war with Britain, was madness. Eventually he faced the inevitable; he committed suicide in his bunker in Berlin on 30th April 1945.

8th October 1939

The parallels between Napoleon, Hitler and Stalin are obvious since each had set about massively expansionist adventures, initially successful but later waging insane war and demanding victory at any cost. Whether Hitler would end up defeated and imprisoned was not yet clear.

TELL THAT TO THE MARINES, ADOLF!

10ᵗʰ December 1939

Hitler's attempts to present himself and the Nazi machine as reasonable agents of peace and prosperity who were bringing a bright future to the nations that they defeated were almost laughable. His efforts to portray Soviet Russia, with whom Germany had agreed a pact of non-aggression (and which was then broken), as a villain didn't get him far either; while doubtless Stalin was a less then beneficent leader, the League of Nations wasn't about to let Hitler off the hook.

WAITING FOR SANTA!

◀ 24th December 1939

Hitler's megalomania was akin to the behaviour of a spoiled and demanding child. The unfortunate fact was that Hitler, while prone to temper tantrums and irrationality, also had access to one of the mightiest war machines the world has ever seen, and thus, until the Allies began to win the war, the pursuit of his aims often meant annihilation for the unfortunate souls who defied him.

THE THREE WISE MONKEYS !

▲ 21st January 1940

The British Government's policy towards Hitler in the late 1930s, a policy of negotiation and non-engagement, appalled many people as the Germans became more belligerent and invaded the Sudetenland area of Czechoslovakia in 1938. Chamberlain's September 1938 "Peace in Our Time" speech, during which he brandished the paper Hitler had signed promising peace, was to prove overly optimistic; six months later the Germans invaded the rest of Czechoslovakia in defiance of the agreement. The first six months of the war saw little real fighting between Britain and Germany and is often referred to as "the Phoney War".

"HERE YOU ARE ADOLF, YOU'RE NEEDING SCRAP IRON — IT'S BEEN CLUTTERING UP MY BACKYARD FOR DAYS..!!"

25th February 1940

The destruction of Germany's highly effective submarine U-boats was of crucial importance to the British war effort. Key in this respect was the battleship *Graf Spee*. After months of attacking Allied shipping in the south Atlantic, she was badly damaged in an engagement with three British cruisers in December 1939 and forced to put into port at Montevideo in neutral Uruguay for repairs. Her captain believed (wrongly) that the British aircraft carrier *Ark Royal* and battle cruiser *Renown* were waiting offshore for him to emerge, and so scuttled his ship in the River Plate estuary before committing suicide.

"WELL, AT LEAST WE'RE STILL SAFE — WE HOPE...!!"

3rd March 1940

As the storm clouds gathered, the Scandinavian nations felt that neutrality was the best policy. In the event their faith was to prove unfounded. Hitler invaded and quickly overran Norway in April 1940, a crucial strategic point to ensure safety for his navy in the Baltic. Denmark was given an ultimatum that it could not refuse, and was taken with only token resistance. Sweden fared better, managing to remain neutral throughout the war, although this was at the cost of assisting the Axis powers by allowing troops to transit and supplying goods to both sides.

17th March 1940

The Russian attack on Finland in November 1939 was expected by Stalin to be a swift invasion. The Soviet forces had many more troops, aircraft and tanks than the Finns. However, thanks to the extraordinary commitment and resolve of the Finnish forces, as well as their local knowledge, they succeeded in holding off the brutal Russian assault until March 1940 when Moscow agreed a peace treaty in return for a small amount of Finnish territory. The League of Nations judged the Russian invasion illegal and expelled the Soviet Union.

24th March 1940

In March 1940 the Royal Air Force launched a massive bombing raid on the Sylt seaplane base in Denmark, causing severe damage and destruction to the German aircraft stationed there. The raid, while strategically important in terms of the damage done to the Wehrmacht, was also about restoring pride after the audacious German air attacks on British vessels in Scapa Flow, Orkney, in the previous months.

"RIDE HIM COWBOY...!"

31st March 1940

In 1940 a dispute between Yugoslavia and Romania was arbitrated by the Axis powers and led to the dislocation of ethnic groups, fermenting resentment. The situation became so unstable that Germany occupied Romania. Meanwhile, Mussolini's invasion of Greece was such a shambles that Hitler had to intervene; and since this meant moving his troops through Yugoslavia, he invaded. Despite the German victory, about 300,000 men managed to stay at liberty and fight a guerrilla war under Tito against their occupiers, giving the German Army a very uncomfortable stay in Yugoslavia.

'—ON THE OUTSIDE ALWAYS LOOKING IN..!' PIX

7th April 1940

The dominance of the British Navy was able to stifle shipping through the Baltic Sea into Germany, depriving her of vital supplies and goods from neutral nations. In many battles towards the end of the war German commanders were forced to alter their tactics because they lacked the fuel needed to move their arms and troops around freely.

14th April 1940

The German invasions of Norway and Denmark in 1940 were portrayed by the Nazis as offering these countries protection, but were in reality a bid for assets and strategic advantage in the coming war. After swiftly occupying Norway the Nazis installed Vidkun Quisling as a puppet ruler, whose name is now synonymous with "traitor". However, the Norwegian people continued to strongly resist their invaders throughout the war.

Bravery, Endurance, Fortitude!

31st May 1940

As the Nazi machine swept through the Low Countries in May 1940 and into France, the British Expeditionary Force, which was stationed in Europe, was pinned back on the French coast. Thousands of troops were trapped at Dunkirk, Calais and Boulogne with the mighty German Army in front of them and the sea to their rear. They were rescued in the "Little Boats" operation in which over the period of a week at the end of May 1940 every vessel that could be mustered was sent again and again over the English Channel to evacuate the troops. Despite the Germans' attempts to halt the operation, this rag-tag assembly of craft managed to extract over 300,000 men.

16th August 1940

The heroic action by the RAF in the Battle of Britain led to repeated delays in Hitler's planned amphibious invasion of England. His "Operation Sealion" was postponed again and again, and eventually shelved indefinitely. By failing to subdue Britain, Hitler both committed Germany to fighting on two fronts, in the west and the east, and also showed Britain and the world that he could, and would, be beaten.

20th August 1940

London's position at the end of a large estuary produced challenges for ground-based air defences. One solution was to build a network of towers housing anti-aircraft guns out in the water to attack incoming Luftwaffe aircraft. This, coupled with the skill and bravery of RAF fighter pilots, made Nazi air assaults on London increasingly hazardous: by the end of August 1940 German losses were mounting and the ferocity of her attacks lessening. By the middle of September 1940 the threat of invasion had lifted and the Battle of Britain was over.

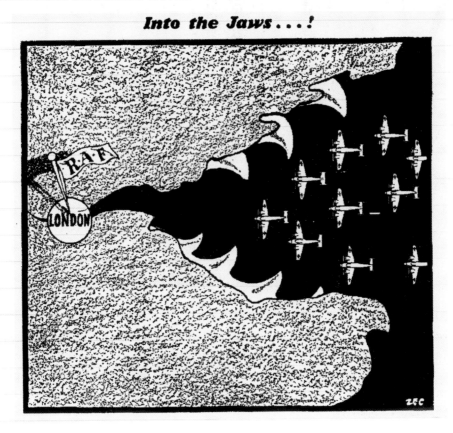

15th September 1940

The full might of the German Luftwaffe was brought to bear upon Britain in early September 1940. Hitler launched a Blitzkrieg of air attacks, intending the massive bombing campaign to bring about swift capitulation. However, despite the ferocity of the onslaught and the loss of life and ensuing damage, Britain remained resolutely defiant and refused to be cowed into surrender. While further bombing continued throughout the war, by May 1941 the Blitz was over. Some 40,000 civilians died, 46,000 were injured and one million homes had been destroyed. But the Luftwaffe had lost 2,400 aircraft and achieved none of their objectives.

"Not on THIS Soil, Hermann!"

30th October 1940

Pierre Laval was a prominent member of the Vichy government, the authority which ran France and her possessions after her armistice with Germany in June 1940. Laval twice served as France's head of state, and regularly acted as a go-between, shuttling between the Vichy government and the Nazis; he was widely seen as a scheming appeaser of the Germans. His negotiations and motives are still the subject of debate and controversy. At the end of the war he was tried and executed for high treason.

AS SUN SETS SO SHADOWS LENGTHEN

J.C. WALKER

20th January 1941

The zenith of Mussolini's premiership in Italy had been the invasion and occupation of Abyssinia (Ethiopia) in 1936 and its re-naming as Italian East Africa. Together with his already held territories of Eritrea and Italian Somaliland he had proclaimed the creation of an Italian East African Empire to jubilant crowds at home. However, when the Allies launched a counter-offensive against the Axis powers in Africa, a combined force including the exiled emperor Haile Selassie ousted the Italian forces from Abyssinia in 1941, restoring Selassie to the throne.

14th February 1941

As the war dragged on and Il Duce's expectation of a swift German victory evaporated in the face of British resistance, the wild adulation he had enjoyed at home began to falter. The Italian defeats in Abyssinia (Ethiopia), Libya and Albania were an embarrassment to the Italian nation and her Axis cohorts. Once Sicily had been retaken in the summer of 1943 and the Germans had retreated to the mainland, Mussolini's position became increasingly precarious. The King bowed to public and political pressure and Mussolini was removed from power. The Italian government agreed an armistice with the Allies in September 1943.

THE UNINVITED GUEST

10th March 1941

Mussolini struggled to convince the Italian public of the wisdom of requesting German assistance in defending his back door in Sicily. The hollowness in his argument that the Germans' presence is for Italy's own good is shown up by the examples of previous "protection" operations, all of which led to occupation.

21st April 1941

Mussolini's attempts to invade Albania and Egypt led to routs. A combination of poor training, communications, supply lines and equipment meant that the Italian forces were relatively easily overcome. Hitler's Axis partner's misadventures were an irritation and embarrassment to him and his plans for the "Pact of Steel" alliance to dominate the western world. The need for Hitler to regularly supply reinforcement for Mussolini's forces became a drain on the Third Reich's resources.

"Can't we be friends?"

16th May 1941

As Hitler's deputy in the early years of the Nazi movement, Rudolf Hess was a significant figure in the Third Reich. On 10th May 1941 Hess flew a twin-engine aircraft to Scotland, evading the pursuing German aircraft, before parachuting to the ground in Renfrewshire. His reported intention was to contact the Duke of Hamilton to negotiate peace between Germany and Britain, but this tactic was not sanctioned by Hitler and did not convince the Allies. He was kept in custody throughout the war, and at the Nuremberg trials was sentenced to life imprisonment. He died in 1987 at Spandau Prison.

28th May 1941

The question which had hung over the world since the start of the war was finally answered on 27th May 1941 when President Roosevelt made a broadcast from the White House proclaiming a national emergency and putting the USA on a war footing. Hitler had been convinced that America would not join the war. Roosevelt's announcement was a tipping point in the war, when the odds swung massively against the Axis powers.

28th May 1941

On 20th May 1941 the German battleship *Bismarck* set out on an attacking foray into the Atlantic. New, fast and heavily armed, she was one of the most formidable ships in the German Navy. Three days out of port she and her escort were engaged by a group of British Navy warships including HMS *Hood*. In the exchanges that followed, the *Hood* was sunk but the *Bismarck* was badly damaged. She was tracked down and sunk on 26th May 1941, inflicting a huge blow to the German fleet and morale.

7th July 1941

The remoteness of the crisis facing Russia in her titanic battle with invading German forces made it easy to forget how important the struggle was to the outcome of the war. Public opinion was roused when things were going badly, but soon subsided as news of a Russian recovery came through. Commentators realized the precariousness of the position and the disastrous consequences if Russia lost the fight. They warned against the dangers of complacency in believing the Russians would prevail and sought to prompt the government into giving greater aid to Stalin.

The First American Casualty.

8th December 1941

On 7th December 1941 Japan mounted an air raid on the US base at Pearl Harbor on Oahu in the Hawaiian Islands. In a two-hour lightning attack hundreds of warplanes bombed the ships and aircraft sitting in the base. Yet the Japanese plan to rob the US military of any ability to strike back was not fully achieved, since, while causing a great deal of damage, they left 20 cruisers, 65 destroyers and, crucially, 3 aircraft carriers intact. And, to Hitler's horror, they had forced America into a declaration of war: this was to prove decisive in the Allied victory four years later.

10th December 1941

The Allies' fortunes against the Japanese invading forces in 1941 and 1942 were not good. The rapid progress of the Imperial Army towards Singapore in December 1941 was resisted until the lack of vital supplies undermined their efforts to oppose the Japanese forces' advance, a plight exacerbated by the poor transport links through a country covered almost entirely in jungle, with few roads or airfields. Although reinforced by four brigades arriving in January 1942, Kuala Lumpur fell on 11th January and by 15th February the Allies had no choice but to surrender.

17ᵗʰ December 1941

The German Army became locked in a stalemate in the autumn of 1941 when faced with determined Soviet opposition at Leningrad and Sevastopol. The German troops were not equipped for harsh winter conditions. With temperatures below minus 20°C, their summer kit, inadequate shelter and lack of food all conspired to demoralize the German forces. Hitler's refusal to sanction a tactical withdrawal to better positions to ride out the winter also diminished German chances of success. The Russian forces, by contrast, had suitable clothing and used the winter lull to bring up reinforcements and equipment ready for the counter-attack.

Russian Ballet!

27th December 1941

Christmas 1941 brought little to cheer the Nazi leadership. Mired on the eastern front by an unexpectedly powerful Soviet force, losing the battle for the seas, failing to conquer Britain, being pounded by bombing raids, struggling to keep the Allies at bay in North Africa and with the USA entering the war, the outlook was uncertain for the previously invincible Wehrmacht.

Seasonal Hangover!

RUNNING COMMENTARY

24th January 1942

General Erwin Rommel was sent to sort out the fiasco being suffered by Mussolini's forces in Libya in February 1941. The Italian forces had suffered heavy defeats to the British and were in disarray. At the time Rommel arrived the Axis position seemed irretrievable; however, he succeeded in turning the fight and winning back territory from the British forces, only to eventually suffer a total defeat.

14th February 1942

In an event dubbed "The Channel Dash" a German Navy squadron set out in February 1942 to run through the British blockade and sail from Brest to Germany through the English Channel. Caught by surprise when the German ships were spotted by two Spitfire pilots, the British response was initially uncoordinated. Along with attacks from motor boats, six aged Fairey Swordfish torpedo bomber aircraft were despatched and mounted an attack. They failed to inflict any damage and all six aircraft were destroyed, killing all crew members.

Valour That Will Bring Final Victory

Members of the gallant Swordfish crews (not one of the aircraft returned) have been awarded medals for valour.

Riding with the New Chauffeur ...

—J. S. Walker Cartoon, "South Wales Echo"

"Boss" Hitler has taken over the wheel of the Nazis' war chariot "going East." . . . Running in third gear, Moscow is as far off as ever. The new Chauffeur has issued a new order of the day . . . "Stand still!" What would he not give if he could stand still? . . . But he's going back!

21st February 1942

The Russians began a counter-offensive against the Germans in December 1941. In the same month Field Marshall von Brauchitsch left the Army High Command due to ill health, allowing Hitler to assume the role as commander-in-chief of the army. Against his generals' advice, Hitler refused to allow any form of tactical withdrawal, forcing his troops to defend poor positions. This led to heavy losses, notably at the village of Mojaisk near Moscow.

2nd March 1942

Starting in late 1941, Japan overran Singapore, Borneo, Java, Sumatra and many other Pacific Islands at amazing speed. Forcing an American surrender from a resolutely held redoubt on the Bataan peninsula led to the capture of the Philippines, a move completed by the surrender of all US defence once their final holding of the island of Corregidor became untenable. Siam (now Thailand) and Burma quickly followed, and by the middle of 1942 Japan had achieved all her targets.

9th March 1942

The seemingly unstoppable advance of the Japanese Imperial Army towards its goal of controlling the whole of Asia, including India, had swept all before it. But even before the attack on Pearl Harbor and the US declaration of war, it was uncertain whether the Japanese could hold on to the newly occupied territories.

26th June 1942

By early 1942 Field Marshal Rommel's Afrika Korps had turned the tables on the Allies after their early successes against the Axis powers in North Africa. Following the fall of Tobruk he swept at lightning speed across the deserts of Libya, winning every engagement and bearing down upon Egypt and the strategically vital Suez Canal. His progress was halted within sight of the Egyptian border at the first battle of El Alamein, which marked the start of the Allied fight back and eventual victory in North Africa.

The right spirit, anyway!

HISTORY'S MOST GLORIOUS PAGES

SEBASTOPOL

SIGNED

29th June 1942

The Ukranian port of Sevastopol, situated on the Crimean peninsula, was the main harbour for Russian Black Sea Fleet. A strategic target for the invading Axis forces during "Operation Barbarossa", it came under heavy attack from the invading forces in October 1941, but the Soviet forces managed to hold the city. They continued to keep the Germans at bay until July 1942, when a huge attack forced it into Hitler's hands. The siege and battle, like so many engagements on the eastern front, cost hundreds of thousands of lives on both sides.

Hors d'oeuvre!

8th August 1942

The Allied raid on the German-occupied French port of Dieppe in August 1942 began at 5am and by 9am a retreat had been called with the loss of over 60% of the 6,000 men who made it ashore. The RAF lost 106 aircraft and the navy suffered over 500 casualties. It was a catastrophe in terms of losses, but it did, however, show that such an assault was possible and taught the Allies some lessons that were put to good use later in the war when the successful D-Day landings were planned and executed.

As dry as a bone!

9th August 1942

As the Russian Army was forced back by the Germans in 1942 they recognized the strategic significance of the oil wells at Maikop falling into enemy hands. The Wehrmacht needed large quantities of fuel to maintain its progress, and this was becoming harder to get as the battle for naval supremacy was tilting in the Allies' favour and the blockade became more effective. Realizing that they must fall back but not wanting Hitler to get his hands on the oil wells, the Russians torched them, depriving the Germans of a vital asset.

Skeleton keys

3rd October 1942

Hitler's invasion of Russia had by this time ground to a halt; the Führer and Stalin ordered that Stalingrad must be theirs – no matter what the cost. By October German forces had succeeded in taking some parts of the virtually ruined city; opposing forces faced each other across a front line amidst the rubble in some places only metres wide. With nearly two million dead, conditions for civilians and soldiers were appalling. The conflict ended when Russia surrounded the city and the German forces were unable to survive on the air-dropped supplies; they surrendered in February 1943.

2nd November 1942

While Hitler's invasion of Russia had stalled in the face of rock hard resistance, the Führer hoped that Japan's Asian adventure would progress and they would overrun China. If this had happened Russia would be forced to divert some resources to defending her eastern border against the Japanese, thus weakening her western front and improving the German Army's chances of making a breakthrough. Japan was unable to make any real progress, however, and remained mired in a conflict with China which had begun in 1937.

HUNTING THE HUNTER

9th November 1942

The Japanese offensive on New Guinea in May 1942 initially went well as Japanese troops moved towards their target of Port Moresby despite strong resistance from the Australian Army. The dense jungle, disease, heat and wildlife combined to make both sides' lives a misery. Yet the Australian resistance and counter-attack were so ferocious that the Japanese were issued the unthinkable order to retreat. It took many months of hard fighting to win back the territory, but the Australians eventually prevailed. This was a great blow to Japanese pride and a fillip to Allied morale.

11th December 1942

The navy's role in the Second World War was crucial. Having withstood severe losses inflicted early on by Germany's U-boats, by 1942 the balance was tipping in the Allies' favour. The fleet was still hunting down U-boats, shelling enemy positions, transporting troops, minesweeping and, perhaps most importantly, providing cover for merchant ships bringing in vital supplies of food, equipment and raw materials across the Atlantic. While Allied shipping losses were heavy, UK and US joint manufacturing output more than offset the lost tonnage: on a net basis the Allied fleet actually increased in size over the first half of the war.

27th December 1942

Having held on in the face of the mighty German onslaught, Russia launched a counter-attack in December 1941. Reinforcing its army with hundreds of thousands of troops, which Germany had thought impossible, and building tanks at a rate faster than the Axis forces could destroy them, the Russians inflicted terrible damage on the invaders. Refused permission to retreat to better positions and with several senior commanders killed, the German Army was suffering badly.

NEW YEAR'S GIFT FROM RUSSIA

"It does this every time I read the news from Russia"

1st January 1943

The privations suffered by both military personnel and the civilian population in Russia during the Second World War were beyond comprehension. Cold and starvation claimed almost as many lives as bombs and bullets. Lack of food drove people to eat their pets, rats and even each other; there were cases of cannibalism in besieged Russian cities. The two armies were commanded by men who refused to retreat one inch, regardless of the human cost.

Invincible Nazi Spread-Eagle!

5th January 1943

Hitler's misadventures, especially amid the snows and stalemate in Russia, made it clear that his war machine was in trouble. Losing the battle for the seas and the air, routed from North Africa and struggling to keep hold of his newly acquired territory, Hitler was a beleaguered soul. It was increasingly clear by early 1943 that the likely outcome of the war was an Allied victory; however, the Nazis' refusal to accept the inevitable led to a further 18 months of conflict and the loss of millions more lives.

A SAIL IN SIGHT

25th January 1943

The terrible struggle that Russia endured to resist the Nazi machine as Hitler sought to occupy the country is almost beyond description. In January 1943 Churchill and Roosevelt met for a conference in Casablanca to strengthen the Allies' alliance. Stalin did not attend as he thought it more important to stay and fight the Germans on Russia's eastern front, but hoped for the Allies to come to his aid. The German attempt to overrun Russia brought 3.4 million German and 4.7 million Russian troops into conflict; the largest engagement in any war in history.

27th January 1943

Forced onto the defensive in the face of Russia's extraordinary resistance and the counter-attack at Stalingrad, the Nazis could only endeavour to hold their position and wait for the Soviet push. It came on 22nd June 1944, three years to the day after Hitler had launched "Operation Barbarossa" against Russia, when the might of the Red Army was unleashed on the Wehrmacht. The German line was quickly broken, signalling the start of a rapid advance by the Russians through the occupied countries and continuing all the way to Berlin.

1st March 1943

Despite their success at Stalingrad, the Russians had not yet turned the invading Axis forces back. Both sides were locked in a stalemate and each planned a spring offensive, hoping it would prove decisive. The warmer weather brought some relief to the troops, although the ice and snow was exchanged for thick mud, which hampered movement.

3rd March 1943

The Axis powers' seizure of swathes of North Africa was started by Mussolini, badly, in 1940 and continued by Rommel, successfully, from 1941 to 1942. The seemingly unstoppable Panzerarmee Afrika were first held by the British 8th Army at El Alamein, almost on the Egyptian border, in July 1942. This success encouraged the Allies and a new leader was drafted in: General Montgomery. Under his leadership the Germans were forced back and lost every major North African engagement thereafter until they were finally expelled from all their previously occupied territory.

16th March 1943

Dr Joseph Goebbels, the Nazi Propaganda Minister, tried to spin events and portray his government and army's actions in a positive light. His attempts to cover up the brutality of the regime's treatment of occupied nations' populations became increasingly far-fetched. The universal experience of German occupation for civilians was one of oppression, intimidation, beatings, forced labour, rape, looting and summary execution on a massive scale. The treatment of those selected for transport to the concentration camps was infinitely worse still.

"We can't make friends, but we can influence people!"

Everywhere the German occupation forces have secured for themselves a particular degree of authority by exemplary behaviour and by consideration for the needs of the defeated nations, as far as this is compatible with the exigencies of war." –GOEBBELS

30th March 1943

With the war turning against the Axis there was disharmony between the various elements of the regime. The reversals in Russia, Abyssinia, China, Libya, Greece and against Britain were beginning to mount up. The situation in France, governed by the puppet Vichy government following the German invasion, was in some doubt as an Allied counter-offensive seemed more and more likely. Plans for a conquest of the world seemed a long way off.

11th May 1943

The Axis powers were beaten and repulsed from Africa not only by the British 8th Army but by forces from all the Allied nations. The navy played a vital part in stifling supply lines to the German and Italian Armies. Once they had been beaten and the North African coast had come under the control of the Allies, the Mediterranean Sea was effectively in Allied hands. This was crucial to Allied efforts to gain a foothold on the European mainland by attacking Italy.

Mediterranean Cruise

9th July 1943

The see-sawing contest between the Russians and Germans saw thrust and counter-thrust being traded between invading and defending forces for three years after the German invasion in 1941. As had their previous assaults, the third German offensive ground to a halt in the face of tough Soviet resistance.

Going down for the third time.

The Aces who never fly.

15th July 1943

While the glory inevitably went to the pilots and aircrew who risked their lives daily against the Luftwaffe and enemy anti-aircraft gunners, the aircraft which they flew and the bombs which they dropped had to be produced in vast quantities under very difficult conditions. The efforts of the men and women who kept the production lines rolling despite the devastating bombing on Britain's manufacturing centres such as Coventry, Bristol and Birmingham, coupled with the privations inflicted by the war on food, fuel and clothing, were nothing short of heroic too.

23rd July 1943

In the late 1930s Benito Mussolini had been impressed by Hitler's regime and his ability to ride roughshod over both Britain and France and retain control of the occupied Sudetenland territory of Czechoslovakia. He believed he was joining up with an unstoppable ally and leading his nation to greatness. By July 1943 his dreams were in tatters and he was forced to leave office. Whether he rued not allying himself with Anthony Eden and Britain instead is uncertain.

Marry in haste . . .
repent at leisure.

Home Guards listen to their instructions
before going out on patrol in 11th July 1941.

"Relatives Of Casualties Have Been Informed"

2nd August 1943

Recalling the famous poster "Careless Talk Costs Lives", the open discussion of Allied plans could put troops' lives in jeopardy if crucial details about impending operations were discovered by our foes. Some irresponsible people "in the know" were overheard talking about the imminent drop of forces into German-held France; this was the cause of great concern.

19th August 1943

The appalling damage brought on Britain by the German Blitzkrieg bombing in the early stages of the war had not been forgotten when in 1943 the Allies had achieved air superiority over the Nazis. A change in tactics from limiting targets only to military installations, to allowing carpet-bombing of entire cities, led to the all-out strategic bombing of Germany. During the first eight months of 1943 an incredible amount of ordnance was dropped on German cities: 11,000 tons on Hamburg, 8,000 tons on Essen, 6,000 tons each on Duisburg and Berlin and 5,000 tons each on Düsseldorf and Nuremberg.

The Debt-collector.

Image text: "I AM AT HEART, A SIMPLE ARCHITECT." Hitler. 1939

26th November 1943

The Allied bombing of Germany brought ruin to many of her finest cities. The Luftwaffe was intended to be a weapon used for the short, sharp action of Blitzkrieg, and used to attack tactical targets. Early in the war Hitler ordered the cessation of design work on new military aircraft since they would not be needed after the war. The Allies' use of air power as a weapon to destroy not only military targets and the means of weapon production, but also towns, cities and morale, brought widespread devastation to parts of the Fatherland.

Man Doomsday!

7th December 1943

The Allies began their campaign to retake Europe by launching an invasion of Sicily on 10th July 1943. Having been softened up for the previous month by bombing and shelling, Italian defences both on the island and mainland were in disarray and Hitler had done little to respond to Mussolini's requests for help other than promise secret weapons. This, coupled with the Axis powers' belief that the Allies would attempt to take Sardinia, aided the British and American forces to take the island on 17th August 1943. It was to become a toe-hold in Europe from which the liberation of Italy could begin.

20th December 1943

A mood of greater confidence was in the air by Christmas 1943, with events turning more and more in the Allies' favour and the future for the Axis powers looking bleaker. While victory was more than a year away, it seemed at last within their grasp.

A TREE-T IN STORE

OF COURSE, IT WILL LOOK A LOT MORE CHRISTMASSY NEXT YEAR, WHEN WE HANG UP THE DECORATIONS.

1st January 1944

At the end of 1943 Rommel had been sent by Hitler to reinforce Germany's defences along the French coast in anticipation of an Allied landing to come. Come it did with "Operation Overlord" being launched on the night of 5th/6th June 1944. The D-Day landings attacked the German defences with 130,000 troops, 4,000 vessels and 13,000 aircraft. Despite determined resistance and massive losses, the Allied forces successfully progressed from the beaches, pushed the Germans back and established a stronghold in Normandy that would be the base for the eventual liberation of Europe.

Leap Year.

1st March 1944

Whether Hitler ever really tried to bargain for his freedom as the Allies closed in on him is uncertain. However, treachery and insincerity marked his dealings throughout his career after he rose to power in the early 1930s. The deaths of Hitler and Mussolini deprived the Allies of the chance to bring them to justice, though a great many members of the Nazi leadership were brought to trial after the war at Nuremberg.

5th March 1944

As the Germans prepared to invade Russia, Finland began to cooperate with them and participated in the siege of Leningrad against the Russian defenders. In June 1944 the Russians again attacked Finland, which was assisted by Germany to defend herself. Russia failed again and peace was agreed on condition that Finland expel the German troops from Lapland, which they duly did. Bulgaria aligned itself with the Axis powers and occupied parts of Greece and Yugoslavia, until in 1944 it was invaded by Russia. This enabled the Bulgarian Communists to seize power, and they turned the Bulgarian forces against Germany.

" We like it here—it's handy for getting out ! "

"S-S-Stop s-s-saying 'S-S-Say W-When'!"

21st April 1944

With the Allies in control of the seas and the skies and making progress through Italy and with the Russian front finally falling in favour of Stalin, it was clear that a liberating force would be launched to retake France. The Allies succeeded in concealing the time, nature and place of the attack from the Germans, keeping them guessing and preventing the reinforcement of the point of attack, Normandy, until it was too late.

5th June 1944

"Operation Overlord", the landings on the Normandy coast, in June 1944 was a success thanks to the bravery and commitment of thousands of troops. Faced with massive German defensive firepower, many men were cut down before they left the beaches. Those who made it to the cliff tops had to clear enemy positions by grenade, flamethrower and bullet. Once the coast had been secured the fight to liberate Europe and force the German Army back until the Allies and Russia met in Berlin in May 1945 was to last many weary months of hard-fought battle for every yard of soil.

There's a long, long trail a-winding . . .

3rd July 1944

Late on in the war victory for the Allies was regarded as only a matter of time. The Nazi machine was in retreat and increasingly desperate to turn the tide. They began to release propaganda declaring the imminent threat of new and devastating super weapons to terrorize the Allies. When these weapons failed to appear the mood at home turned to derision; here Hitler is lampooned as he considers a daft invention, which also parodies the weakness of the German military at that point in the war.

4th July 1944

Hitler's designers finally created an unmanned flying bomb capable of reaching distant targets with reasonable accuracy. The V1, or doodlebug, was fired at Britain from June 1944, targeting London primarily. Many reached their targets, causing great damage, injury and death. However, by the end of August the British defence forces had become expert at shooting them down from the coast and the threat receded, only to be replaced by the larger, faster V2, 500 of which landed on the London area. Despite the carnage they wrought, Hitler's intention to break the spirit of the civilian population was not realized.

There is no weak link.

"Heard any goot vuns about Vorld Domination?"

5th July 1944

The Russian advance westwards after the battle of Stalingrad was lightning fast; the front had moved 400 miles between July and September 1944. The Axis forces were in full flight, with 25 of the 37 divisions of the German Army Group Centre annihilated. The losses were so severe that on 5th October all youths of 16 years old were conscripted and all hospitals deemed under military control. The Volkssturm was created; a peoples militia to defend the Fatherland.

Intuition

11th July 1944

As it became clear that Hitler was bent on continuing an unwinnable war at awful cost to the nation, a plan to assassinate him was hatched within German senior ranks. In July 1944 Staff Officer Colonel Count Claus von Stauffenberg placed a bomb under a table where Hitler was holding a meeting. The explosion killed four people, but only succeeded in blowing Hitler's trousers off and inflicting minor injury. The resulting purge of Hitler's staff effectively ended the resistance movement but also weakened the Nazi war machine since a number of senior staff, including several generals, were removed from office or executed.

13th July 1944

It was obvious that the Russian Army was not going to be stopped and was preparing to enter Germany. Terrified of a Bolshevik invasion, and the consequent swapping of one tyrant for another, thousands of German refugees fled west towards the advancing Allies. The legendary German commander Field Marshall Rommel was found to have been complicit in the Stauffenberg bomb plot and committed suicide rather than stand trial, depriving Hitler of his master tactician when the threat to his country was greatest.

Bedtime Story

Harvesting time

30th July 1944

The Russian Army was reinvigorated after the years of stalemate between it and the invading German Army when they launched their June 1944 summer offensive. Assisted by equipment sent by the USA and Britain, they hurled themselves at the German forces. The Germans were poorly supplied and compelled to follow increasingly irrational orders from Hitler. They were quickly overrun and their entire line broken from north to south. The Russians pushed quickly through Poland and East Prussia.

23rd August 1944

During the second half of 1944 the German Army was also pushed back through Lithuania, Estonia, Hungary, Bulgaria, Czechoslovakia, Romania, Albania, Greece and Yugoslavia. The German retreats, evacuations and withdrawals towards their homeland with Hitler's orders to fight to the last made it clear that victory would not be assured until the leaders of the Third Reich were either dead or captured – and that would mean an assault on Berlin.

"If we're going to fight to the last man we'd better start finding some humans!"

"Now Paris IS an Open City."

24th August 1944

Once the Allies had secured Normandy after the D-Day landings, the breakout and liberation of France began. Although Eisenhower intended to simply bypass Paris on the push towards Germany, at the insistence of General De Gaulle the Allies permitted it to be liberated by French forces. On 25th August 1944 they were in the suburbs of the city and by the following day Paris had been freed. General von Cholitz, the Nazi commander in charge of the city, and his colleague General Spiedel both disregarded Hitler's spiteful orders to raze the city to the ground before surrendering it.

"Ah, Prof. Schnitzel, if only we could make *that* one!"

1st September 1944

Hitler's secret weapons planners brought to life the V1 and V2 flying bombs. They had also built, but not managed to make fully functional, a V3 weapon. This multiple shell-launching 50-barrelled super gun was sited near Calais. It was theoretically capable of raining a shell every few minutes on London. However, its projectiles tended to tumble in flight, making them inaccurate and short of range, and it was never used against the Allies before it was captured after the Normandy breakout in the autumn of 1944.

3rd September 1944

A great many German defensive lines had fallen during the course of the war: the Mareth
Line in southern Tunisia, the Tunis Line in northeastern Tunisia, the Gustav Line through the
Apennine mountains in Italy, the Adolf Line (later called the Senger Line by Hitler to minimize the
propaganda potential should it be broken) also in Italy, and the Marne Line in France.

"Vot about US hanging out some vashing?"

◀ 6th September 1944

In the 1930s Hitler had constructed a 390-mile long defensive network of bunkers, tanktraps and fortifications opposite the French Maginot Line from the border with the Netherlands to Switzerland. The Nazis called it the Westwall, the Allies referred to it as the Siegfried Line. The fortifications were intended to make Germany invulnerable to attack from the west; however, once it was reached in August 1944 the Allies' superior air power and enormous ground strength meant that it was eventually breached by 1945, permitting the final push towards Berlin.

▼ 7th September 1944

Germany has a poor record of making belligerent attacks on her neighbours from the mid-nineteenth to mid-twentieth centuries. The treachery and crimes against humanity perpetrated by the Nazi machine had appalled the Allied nations. Their view that there was something deeply amiss in the German psyche that compelled her to seek world domination by means of force was a popularly held one. As the war ground towards its conclusion many felt that she should be left so crippled that she could never pose a threat again.

"Himmel! Am I to be interrupted for another twenty years?"

26th September 1944

Hitler's despotic plans to bring the world under Nazi control and the appalling measures employed by the Third Reich towards that goal were sufficient to make most people think that the death penalty was appropriate for him and his henchmen. However, while rumours of such atrocities had circulated for some time, it wasn't until the Allies liberated the concentration camps at the end of the war that the full scale of the crimes committed by the Nazis were revealed.

"*Read this Adolf—it's a later edition*"

The Landing

29th September 1944

Following the great success of the Allied landings and invasion of France and Belgium, progress had slowed when faced with the strong defensive positions taken up by the German Army in Holland. In order to break the deadlock and hasten the end of the war, the Allies launched "Operation Market Garden", an airborne assault on Arnhem aimed at seizing territory and, crucially, bridges, to allow the movement of troops and equipment. In the event it was a failure; German resistance was stronger than expected and thousands of Allied troops were either killed or captured.

A little "swing" music in the Kremlin!

11th October 1944

As the war in Europe ended so came the realization by the world of the full scale of the atrocities committed by the Nazis. With the Allies advancing from the west and Russians from the east, Berlin's fall and the collapse of the Third Reich led to a scramble to escape by senior figures within the Third Reich. Some senior Nazis escaped, but many were captured and tried at an International Court in Nuremberg. Although some pre-empted justice by committing suicide, many were sentenced to death and executed.

1st November 1944

The much anticipated, and for a long time regarded as certain, German invasion of Britain failed to materialize. By late 1944 the threat was so diminished that the Home Guard was stood down. Thankfully their mettle was never directly tested by the Germans and members of the guard were able to hang up their rifles and return fully to civilian life.

"Well, he can't say I didn't wait!"

4th December 1944

Perhaps a more popularly held image of the Home Guard, which later spawned the *Dad's Army* television comedy series, was one of a group of aging and bumbling old duffers. While doubtless resolute and ready to do their all to defend the country, it is highly debateable whether they would have managed to hold back the might of the Nazi Wehrmacht had that invasion ever come.

IN JUNE 1940 WE OLD SWEATS ANSWERED CHURCHILL'S CALL TO THE DEFENCE OF OUR COUNTRY. WE WERE SUPPOSED TO ACT AS SCOUTS WITH SPECIAL KNOWLEDGE OF OUR OWN PARTICULAR DISTRICT.

BUT IT WAS NOT LONG BEFORE WAR OFFICE STARTED MUCKING US ABOUT, AND AFTER ISSUING TAILOR-MADE DENIMS, AND CATCH-AS-CATCH-CAN HEAD GEAR

WE WERE INSTRUCTED IN THE ART OF USING WHITEHALL'S SECRET WEAPONS.

LATER WHEN THE IMMEDIATE FEAR OF INVASION HAD PASSED WE GOT TIN HATS, BATTLE DRESS AND RIFLES, AND WERE TAUGHT HOW TO MAKE OURSELVES PART OF THE LANDSCAPE.

THEN, WHEN OUR ARMY HAD MADE A SUCCESSFUL INVASION OF THE CONTINENT, WE WERE ISSUED WITH UNLIMITED AMMO! BUT BEFORE WE COULD USE IT, WE WERE GIVEN OUR BOWLER HATS

AND A GOODBYE AND FAREWELL FROM WAR OFFICE IN RECOGNITION OF OUR SERVICES.

Autobiography of a Home Guard

By J. C. Walker

Seasonal hangover

27th December 1944

Pushed back to the German border by the Allied advance, Hitler's forces sought to turn the tide of the war with a bold attack. In December 1944 they succeeded in forcing a bold thrust into Belgium, forcing the Allied front back at that point and giving the action its name "The Battle of the Bulge". The Germans' celebrations were short lived, however. By the end of the month they had been pushed back again by General Patton's US Army and Hitler's defeat was only a matter of time.

11th January 1945

When the US Army was forced to surrender their final hold on the Philippines in April 1942 General MacArthur had been ordered to leave for Australia, announcing as he left "I will be back." He made good on that promise when the US began to invade the Philippines in October 1944, steadily liberating it island by island. The Japanese Navy had been pulverized and their ability to defend territory was severely damaged by the end of the year; however, they had 250,000 men and instructions to hold the island of Luzon at all costs. After months of bloody struggle it was liberated in March 1945.

"Says he's got a date he made with you in 1942!"

1ˢᵗ March, 1945

In the wake of the V2 rockets, claims of further nasty surprises continued to emanate from the crumbling Nazi machine. Although none of the promised super weapons ever materialized, had Hitler not been denied the use of the Norwegian heavy water processing plant in Telemark by a daring Allied commando raid to sabotage it early in the war, he might well have had a nuclear bomb by 1945.

"This trick
will have to be
ruddy marvellous."

13th March 1945

As the Allies closed in on Berlin from the west, the last major natural obstacle was the River Rhine. The assault to cross the Rhine was mounted in several places simultaneously, stretching the Nazi forces, which were also engaged with the advancing Russians from the east. Their ability to prepare and react was further hampered by a massive aerial assault by Allied bombers, which kept up a constant barrage of attack on German positions, generating chaos and disrupting communications. The Rhine was crossed in March 1945, allowing Allied troops and equipment to pour across and launch the final assault on Berlin.

20th April 1945

Russia's counter-offensive started deep in their own territory, with the German capital a long way off. Initially the Germans regarded the threat of Berlin being taken a distant one, and Hitler expected his forces to prevail. But the final push by the Allies at the end of the war became a dash for the honour of taking Berlin, one which Russia claimed when her troops raised the Hammer and Sickle on the Reichstag at the end of April 1945.

Joe Gets Going

By J. C. Walker

1st May 1945

After months of dogged progress pushing the Axis armies north through Italy, the weary and demoralized enemy was forced to finally surrender on 2nd May 1945, following many smaller surrenders during the preceding month. Fleeing with the German Army was the deposed Benito Mussolini. On 27th April 1945 he was identified by Italian partisans as he tried to flee from Lake Como to Spain. He was summarily executed and his body hung upside down at a petrol station in Milan as an act of retribution and a warning to his followers.

Here endeth another lesson.

1st May 1945

By May 1945 it had become clear that Hitler was dead and the abhorrent organization he had created was in its death throes. However, even at the hour of triumph of right over wrong, there was fear that the ideals of the Nazis might live on and spring up again in the future. Sadly, the lust for power, greed, racial hatred and inhumanity have characterized many conflicts since the end of the Second World War, and the concern that fascism would not die with the Führer proved well founded.

Where now?

8th May 1945

With Hitler dead and the Third Reich in ruins, the inevitable was finally accepted by Germany on 8th May 1945, with the agreement to surrender to the Allies and end all hostilities in Europe. To worldwide rejoicing, victory had been achieved in Europe and peacetime rebuilding could begin. The conflict still raged with Japan, but this was only a few months away from its conclusion.

"Here you are! Don't lose it again!"

9th May 1945

The jubilation that greeted the May 1945 victory over Germany was not shared by Japan, which refused to surrender and fought on. As the summer of 1945 progressed, Allied forces secured Burma and the last Japanese-occupied islands of Iwo Jima and Okinawa. Fighting was ferocious, with Japanese defenders preferring death to capture, and regarding surrender as unthinkable. Commanders committed *hara-kiri*, honourable suicide, rather than give in, and US warships were subject to repeated *kamikaze*, or suicide aircraft attacks.

"No Hon. celebration—but what an Hon. headache!"

16th May 1945

The struggle between its Japanese occupiers and the 14th Army to liberate Burma had ground on since 1942 until late 1944 without any conclusion. The war in the distant jungle was very different from that in Europe; the vegetation, insects, heat and an enemy that would rather die than retreat made conditions very difficult for the Allies. Launched in late 1944, the Allies' final advance through Burma was a long and arduous struggle until Rangoon was finally liberated in May 1945, leaving only Japan itself to be defeated.

Heil, Mikado!

Bubble . . .

and squeak!

26th May 1945

Joachim von Ribbentrop was a close associate of Hitler from the early 1930s. He was sent to London as German Ambassador in 1936 to negotiate a pact between Britain and Germany. Though associating himself with a number of Germanophile aristocrats, he made no headway with the Foreign Office or MPs. Yet on the basis of his belief that a pact was in the offing, Hitler felt sure Britain would not present any meaningful opposition to his plans. Subsequently recalled to Germany and given the role of Minister of Foreign Affairs in the Third Reich, Ribbentrop was tried at Nuremberg and executed.

"Any Hon. questions?"

10th August 1945

With the war in Europe won, the Allies' full attention turned on Japan. Russia declared war on Japan, honouring a commitment to the Allies, and began an offensive in Manchuria. Heavy bombing of Japanese mainland targets continued throughout May, June and July 1945 without producing a surrender. On 6th August 1945, the US Air Force dropped the world's first nuclear bomb on Hiroshima.

11th August 1945

The scale of the devastation at Hiroshima, and that which followed a further atomic bomb detonation above Nagasaki three days later, had never been seen before. Facing this, coupled with the Russian threat and unable to contemplate the systematic destruction of his country, Emperor Hirohito agreed to surrender on 9th August 1945. Victory over Japan, VJ Day, marked the end of the Second World War.

SET.

16th August 1945

After winning the war against all odds and earning himself the highest esteem in his country and the world for his inspirational leadership and courage, Winston Churchill lost the General Election which was held in July 1945. Boosted by the votes of returning servicemen, there was a swing against the Conservative Party and Labour secured a shock victory. Clement Attlee took over as Prime Minister of postwar Britain. Churchill returned to power in 1951.

'Thank you for light in the darkest hours."

The Wise Men followed only one. . . .

20th December 1945

With the war over, work on reshaping the world began. At the Moscow Conference of Foreign Ministers in October 1945, Byrnes, Bevin and Molotov representing the USA, Britain and Russia respectively, met to discuss the future of Italy, Romania, Bulgaria, Hungary, Finland, Japan, Korea, and China and also the establishment of the United Nations to control atomic energy. Here Zec identifies the issue which has dogged world politics ever since: the self-interest of individual parties. Almost as soon as the Allied troops and nations joined in celebration at their joint victory, their governments began to split and embark on the Cold War.

A street party in the Newton Heath district of Manchester during VE Day celebrations, 8th May 1945.

Also available

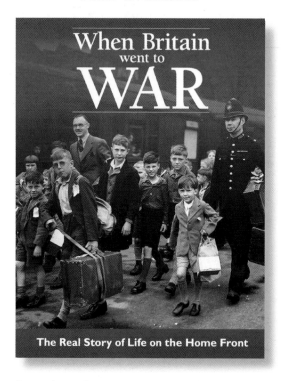

"A nation that forgets its past has no future."
Winston Churchill

When Britain Went To War everyone in the country was involved, whether they were in the military or civilians whose jobs were vital to the war effort. Additionally, every woman in the country, whether a mother, sister, grandmother or daughter was caught up in the conflict. They helped to maintain the everyday life for which Britain's military men were fighting.

This is the real, the everyday story of British men, women and children who fought a daily battle to keep the home fires burning When Britain Went To War.